GETTING A JOB IN
THE TRANSPORTATION
INDUSTRY

KATHERINE YAUN

Published in 2017 by The Rosen Publishing Group, Inc.

29 East 21st Street, New York, NY 10010
Copyright © 2017 by The Rosen Publishing Group, Inc.

First Edition

Library of Congress Cataloging-in-Publication Data

Names: Yaun, Katherine, author.
Title: Getting a job in the transportation industry / Katherine Yaun.
Other titles: Job basics, getting the job you need.
Description: First edition. | New York : Rosen Publishing, [2017] | Series:
 Job basics: getting the job you need | Includes bibliographical
 references. | Audience: 7-12.
Identifiers: LCCN 2016006635 | ISBN 9781477785683 (library bound)
Subjects: LCSH: Transportation—Vocational guidance—Juvenile literature. |
 Transport workers—Juvenile literature.
Classification: LCC HE152 .Y38 2016 | DDC 388.023—dc23
LC record available at http://lccn.loc.gov/2016006635

Manufactured in China

CONTENTS

INTRODUCTION

You are sitting in class itching to move. Suddenly, you hear the distant sound of an airplane. Soon, you hear a train whistle blowing. You think about the large locomotive thundering through town and wonder where it is heading. Just then, a big truck honks as it rolls down the street outside. The roar of an airplane engine, the high whistle of a train, and the honk of an eighteen-wheeler's horn: these are the sounds of people and cargo in transit.

These sounds break your concentration on the lesson in class, but they get you thinking about being a part of the complex web of transportation and logistics that keeps society moving.

The good news is that with the right training and certification you can get moving, too. Being part of the thousands of pilots, railroad engineers, truck drivers, and sailors out there is a realistic goal, if you apply yourself early on and get moving.

People who work in the transportation industry work in four areas: air, rail, ground, and water transportation. This means that they do most of their job duties in the sky, along a railroad track, on the highway, or out on open waterways. Workers in the transportation industry are curious and adventurous. They enjoy seeing new places and meeting new people. They can be both comfortable with routine, yet enjoy a different schedule and set of experiences.

Container ships and eighteen-wheel trucks work together to unload cargo at a port in Peru. Worldwide, the land, water, rail, and air transportation sectors often coordinate in order to move goods and people.

Making a career in the transportation industry can be a stimulating and exciting experience. It is one of the oldest industries, dating back to ancient civilizations. Long ago, people traded things like silk, tea, and cotton. They walked through deserts, climbed mountains, and crossed oceans to sell these things to other people. They used their own backs, horses, and ships to carry them.

Nowadays, international trade networks move consumer items and natural resources ike oil, cars, and computers. Transportation is an old and stable industry, one that experts predict will continue to be strong in the future.

Can you picture a job in the transportation industry in your own future? There are many options to choose from. Air traffic controllers, airline flight attendants, baggage handlers, truck drivers, and many others comprise this dynamic sector, and each job utilizes many different skills.

To get moving, you need the right education, certifications, and perseverance. It is a process that you can start now, before you ever start looking for a job. You can start by learning as much as you can about the industry, applying yourself in school, and making contacts with individuals who work in transportation. By working hard toward your goal, you will be out from behind your desk in no time and speeding toward a promising future in transportation.

CHAPTER ONE

The Sky Is the Limit: Air Transportation

The main purpose of air transportation is to move people and cargo from one place to another quickly. Did you know that it takes about 33 hours to travel the 2,400 miles from the Pacific Ocean to the Atlantic Ocean driving nonstop in a car? In an airplane, it only takes 6 hours. This makes air an ideal way to travel for many people and for businesses and other institutions to move goods.

Air transportation employees work both up in the sky and down on the ground. Inside aircraft you will find helicopter and airplane pilots, copilots, and flight attendants. On the ground, you will find the workers who keep everyone up in the sky safe and organized. These jobs on the ground include air traffic controllers, mechanics, and airport workers. The workplace for these jobs can vary: a control tower, a hangar, or out on a busy runway surrounded by roaring airplane engines.

Careers in air transportation are great for those who enjoy flying, planning, and meeting other people. Air transportation workers like to use their organization skills to plan the most efficient way to move people and cargo. It can feel exhilarating to help direct and land a helicopter as it brings

It takes hundreds of transportation workers to keep the air traffic running smoothly at busy transit hubs like the Los Angeles International Airport (LAX), one of the busiest airports in the world.

someone to a hospital for a lifesaving procedure.

Challenges involved in air transportation include following a strict schedule and working with upset people when travel schedules change due to bad weather or other factors. In general, however, you can expect to earn a good wage and feel satisfaction doing many different jobs in air transportation. The future is promising for a career in air transportation since people will always want and need to travel to points distant for business and pleasure alike. The career options in air transportation are also many and varied. As the old saying goes, "The sky's the limit!"

Things Are Looking Up: Jobs in the Air

There are many jobs in air transportation that take place

onboard aircraft. Much of one's work takes place thousands of feet up in the sky.

Pilots

Pilots might be the first personnel that come to mind when we think of air transportation. Pilots are responsible for the safe takeoff, flight, and landing of an aircraft. This involves having a strong sense of direction, knowledge of how to work the electronic and digital controls inside the aircraft, and ability to communicate with people on and off the aircraft. Pilots carefully record details about what happened during each flight in a special document called a flight record.

Airplane pilots usually work for large commercial airlines and fly short, routine distances within the United States and North America. Other pilots work for airlines that travel longer distances on international routes. It can be exciting to work as a commercial airline pilot and visit so many places.

Helicopter pilots often work for hospitals to transport sick people. They also work for news agencies to film and report traffic and weather patterns. Many helicopter pilots work for themselves or for tourism companies to offer passengers helicopter sightseeing tours.

Airline pilots, either working independently, or for others, are often hired by private parties, too. These are called charter flights. Charter pilots transport small groups of people to see popular destinations and sights such as around city harbors or to nearby mountains. Some charter pilots operate smaller aircraft in order to deliver goods, mail, and other cargo to remote destinations. Sometimes, they even help to put out forest fires.

Pilots who fly for commercial airlines always fly with at least one other person. They work closely with one or more copilots, flight attendants, and air traffic controllers to get the plane to its destination safely.

All branches of the U.S. military—the Air Force, Navy, Army, Marine Corps, and Coast Guard—employ airplane and helicopter pilots. In fact, the U.S. military is the nation's largest employer and hires thousands of people to do transportation-related jobs.

Requirements to Be a Pilot

Becoming a pilot takes hard work and dedication. When you are in high school you can study subjects such as mathematics, computers, electronics, and English. After high school you will either need to join the military for training or obtain a college degree. Once that step is completed, practice is the secret to success. This comes in the form of gaining flight hours, earning your pilot's license, and continuing to pass tests and complete additional training throughout your career.

Attitude and confidence are as important as skill. Flying is not for the faint of heart. Adventurousness, problem-solving skills, and technical know-how are also job prerequisites.

Flight Attendants

Flight attendants are responsible for the safety and comfort of passengers on commercial airliners. They inform passengers of in-flight safety procedures, such as wearing seat belts and remaining seated when necessary. They also instruct passengers on emergency procedures, how to use an oxygen mask, how to use the seat as a flotation device, where emergency exits are, and how to exit the plane. In emergencies, flight attendants are responsible for getting passengers off of the plane safely.

Flight attendants also make sure passengers are comfortable. They provide passengers with food, beverages, blankets, and even headphones to help them relax and have fun. Lastly, flight attendants convey information from the pilots to the passengers. This might include how long the flight will be, how weather is affecting the flight, and other useful or requested information.

Requirements to Be a Flight Attendant

Prospective flight attendants should have people skills. They should be able to talk with a variety of people from different cultures and lifestyle, convey information clearly, and collect information on customer requests. Most flight attendants also enjoy travelling, planning, and organizing. It is helpful to know a second or even a third language if you are interested in working on international flights.

Flight attendants must complete a course of training with the airline company that hires them, and must hold at least a GED or high school diploma. You might attract employers'

One of the most important jobs of flight attendants is to ensure passenger safety. Here, a flight attendant instructs passengers in how to survive a water landing.

attention if your job application shows that you have completed a Flight Attendant Certification Program. Many community colleges and technical schools offer these certificates. Some colleges and universities offer associate degrees and bachelor's degrees in travel and tourism with a focus on the airline industry.

Jobs on the Ground

There are many workers in the air transportation industry who never leave the ground. They spend all day thinking about people and cargo in the air—or the best way to get them up there.

Air Traffic Controllers

Air traffic controllers work in control towers. Their main duty is to safely manage the flow of aircraft in the air and on the ground. They help pilots avoid crashes with other pilots. Just as there is often heavy traffic on roads, streets, and highways, there can also be a lot of traffic in the air. Air traffic controllers act as the green light, red light, and yellow light, telling pilots when they can go, when they need to change course and wait, and precautions they need to take to avoid crashing into another aircraft.

Air traffic controllers manage the traffic in the sky by using radars, schedules, and altitudes. Radars help air traffic controllers follow the progress of an airplane during its flight. Air traffic controllers assign every airplane a specific time to depart. They also assign them a specific altitude, or height in the sky, at which they are allowed to fly. It is a high-pressure and detail-oriented job.

Once an airplane has safely landed at an airport, air traffic controllers ensure that it arrives at its assigned gate without colliding with other planes that have just landed. Last, air traffic controllers communicate with pilots in the air and help them with routine situations and emergencies. A routine situation might be helping a pilot to change course due to a sudden shift in the weather. An emergency situation might be helping the pilot to find a safe place for the plane to safely land in case of mechanical failure, accident, or criminal or terrorist activity.

Becoming an Air Traffic Controller

Coordinating air traffic can be stressful. People's lives depend on your clear thinking and careful planning. Maintaining your wits under pressure is key. Air traffic controllers should also be tech-savvy, be excellent communicators, and be able to synthesize information like weather patterns and flight locations and then make quick decisions based on these.

In high school, you can study subjects like computers, electronics, English, mathematics, and geography to start your training early. After high school you will need to complete a training program offered by the Federal Aviation Administration (FAA), the federal government agency that serves as the most important regulator of all commercial aviation.

But don't wait too long for this step. You need to have started this training before you turn thirty-one. Air traffic controllers complete many hours of on-the-job training spent observing more experienced air traffic controllers in action.

To get hired, you will need either three years of work experience, a bachelor's degree, or a combination of the two. The largest employer of air traffic controllers in the United States is the FAA. The military also employs air traffic controllers.

Airport Workers: Keeping Things Moving

A whole other subset of jobs are administrative or customer service positions. Without these services, airports would not run smoothly. Inside airports, workers provide essential

An air traffic controller uses digital data to interpret the exact locations of the planes he is tracking. He must ensure they get to their destination safely without colliding.

SO YOU WANT TO BE AN AIR MARSHAL?

Air marshals work for the federal Transportation Security Administration (TSA). Their main job duty is to protect passengers by detecting and confronting criminal activity on board a plane. Sometimes air marshals do this work inside an airport, too. They observe groups of people, and if anything appears suspicious they investigate and take action. Air marshals might have to arrest people if they see a crime take place in front of them, obtain search warrants, or interview witnesses. They compile information for officials. To become an air marshal, it is important to have courage and awareness. Air marshals must complete a special training at an academy, learn how to use a firearm, and pass a psychological exam and evaluation. Some people who enter the training academy have a high school diploma or GED, while others are military veterans or have a college degree in criminal justice. Air marshals must be comfortable travelling many hours per month. They must also maintain a high degree of physical fitness.

services such as security, ticket sales, boarding passes, itinerary changes, wheelchair assistance, baggage management, janitorial work, and food service.

Outside of airports, on and near runways, workers help to load and unload baggage and cargo. This can include pets like cats, dogs, or even farm animals. Outdoor airport workers clean and inspect the cabins, where passengers sit. Outdoor airport workers can also direct airplanes that have just landed or are about to take off. Airline companies also hire many airplane mechanics and engineers to keep the airplane engines operating properly or to fix any broken systems on the plane.

Professional office jobs at an airport include airport operations directors, managers, and assistants. They

A baggage handler transfers luggage to an airplane. It takes coordination speed to move an entire airplane's luggage to the baggage carousel inside the airport.

oversee professional services at the airport. This can include anything from hiring and training workers, scheduling and managing runway construction, supervising air traffic controllers, and managing the supply of gas, oil, and lubricants to the giant airplane gas tanks.

Requirements to Be an Airport Worker

Most airport jobs require a high school education or GED. You need to have a basic understanding of mathematics and scheduling, and be customer-oriented. This takes patience and people skills. Managerial positions require an associate or bachelor's degree.

CHAPTER TWO

All Aboard: Rail Transportation

Rail transportation moves people and cargo by train from one place to another. Many jobs in this sector involve working on or around trains, while inspectors, mechanics, and front-office staff are also integral. Some trains travel long distances above ground—including passenger and freight lines—while others travel shorter distances above and underground. The latter includes rail services that serve as commuter transportation networks within cities, or help link suburban commuters to city centers. Every day, millions of people rely on trains to get where they need to be, while thousands of businesses need reliable deliveries of goods via rail to stay viable and competitive.

The railroad industry has been around for more than 185 years. Experts predict that it will continue to remain a key part of the economy in the future, with a 9.2 percent rate of growth over the coming decade. Older railroad workers, particularly freight rail workers, are expected to retire over the next decade, opening up opportunities for younger employees. Some people who work in the rail transportation industry find the long hours away from home challenging. Many factors, including salary, stability, and love for the job, make up for this shortcoming.

Three Types of Rail Business

The rail industry can be split up into three different sectors: freight rail, passenger rail, and urban, or municipal rail. There are several differences among these subsectors of the rail industry.

A major freight rail company in North America, VIA RailCanada, moves cargo along a track. This train is carrying goods to sell at consumer retail outlets in British Columbia, Canada.

Freight Rail

Freight rail remains critical to commerce, and involves moving bulky, heavy cargo on trains and delivering the goods to customers who ordered them. Anything from airplane and submarine parts to wind turbine engines and even elephants is moved as freight. Prominent American railroad companies include CSX, BNSF Rail Logistics, and Union Pacific Railroad. They transport billions of tons of cargo every year. The cargo is delivered to stations in the United States or to port cities to be shipped to other countries. Cargo also moves in the opposite direction— from overseas and into our own rail transportation networks. If you like working around heavy machinery and seeing the direct results of your hard work, you might fight satisfaction being employed in freight rail.

Passenger Rail

Passenger railroads move people. Rail travel can be cheaper and more exciting than air travel. Passenger rail includes train trips from one city to another or from one state to another. In fact, some rail lines offer cross-country passenger rail trips. You can sleep on the train in what's called a sleeper car while going all the way from California to Florida. People use passenger rail to get to their destinations, for social purposes, or simply for a unique vacation experience. If you like helping people get to their destinations, passenger rail could be the career path for you.

Commuter/Municipal Rail

Commuter or municipal rail systems convey passengers in and out of city centers. This includes work and lesiure travel. The former includes commuters going to and from work. Commuter rail passengers also use it as a convenient way to reach concerts, nightlife, and other recreational destinations, and to take care of errands.

Underground urban rail systems are called subways. If you live in a big city, you may have taken a subway or similar train today. Trams, trolleys, and streetcars are other types of vehicles that are lumped in under the bigger umbrella of commuter sytems. If you like the idea of working in a big city, urban rail

A conductor on a New York City Metropolitan Transit Authority (MTA) train looks down the subway platform to make sure people are getting on and off safely.

could be a perfect fit for you. Even though there are three types of rail business, each hires people to do similar jobs. These jobs are on trains, outdoors on and near railroad tracks, in rail yards, and in office support positions.

Conductors and Engineers

Two of the best-known jobs in the railroad industry are railroad engineers and railroad conductors, two jobs often confused with each other. In a nutshell, railroad engineers operate the machinery needed to move a train, while railroad conductors direct all of the people and cargo on a train. Each job's workday is spent mainly on trains.

Railroad engineers typically operate one of two engine types: a diesel locomotive engine or, less often, a battery- or electricity-powered locomotive engine. Before a trip, they check out the engines to make sure everything is working properly. In transit, they are constantly monitoring different controls: airbrakes, speed gauges, throttles, air pressure gauges, battery power, and more. It is a lot to do at once. Needless to say, one of the top qualities for railroad engineers is the ability to multitask.

Railroad conductors are responsible for all of the passengers, crew, and cargo on a train. This can mean coordinating schedules, monitoring railroad track switches, making sure a freight delivery is made on time, and overseeing movement of individual train cars once a train has arrived inside a rail yard. Railroad conductors are in charge of a special list called a waybill, which is a list of passengers or goods being carried on a train. If they are assigned to a passenger rail line, they are responsible for making sure all of the passengers are comfortable and safe. Conductors make announcements, coordinate crew activities, and oversee tickets and fares. One of the top qualities of a railroad conductor is communication with all kinds of people.

Conductors and engineers also rely on electrical monitoring equipment and communication. Railroad engineers focus on interpreting and following orders that affect the train's movement. Railroad conductors typically report information about equipment problems to rail yards or traffic control centers.

Engineers and Conductors

People who work as railroad conductors and railroad engineers are good with technology. They like maintaining and operating equipment. They also tend to be social people who enjoy talking with others and solving problems.

Railroad workers should be social and be able to communicate with a diverse range of people. Here, an Amtrak train conductor gives passengers information during a train delay.

Locomotive engineers need to be federally licensed to operate a train. This is unique in the railroad industry—not every job requires a federal license. But it is common due to the technical expertise and safety needs of both employees and passengers. To earn the license, engineers complete a formal engineer training program approved by the Federal Railroad Administration. The program is usually offered by a railroad company and involves attending classes, driving simulated trains, and doing hands-on training. It requires candidates to pass several exams before they are officially certified, including a hearing and sight test, locomotive operation test, and skills performance test.

Railroad conductor jobs are considered senior positions in the industry. Most railroad conductors start out by working as brake operators, switch operators, or other rail laborers. While they do these jobs, they learn about operating rules, regulations, safety, schedules, signals, and rail equipment. This knowledge helps to prepare them to become conductors in the future. Conductors might complete some training offered by a railroad company or a community college. Students usually finish these programs with a railroad conductor technology certificate.

To start preparing now, you can study subjects like algebra, industrial arts, physics, geometry, and driver's education. You can also decide now which type of rail business you are most interested in (freight, passenger, or urban) and start learning more. Look online to learn more about the many opportunities available in rail. Freight rail, especially, are especially well compensated, with an average salary with benefits for senior and veteran employees running about $107,000 annually, according to the Association of American Railroads.

HIGH-SPEED RAIL AND GREEN TRANSPORTATION

High-speed rail is one solution for a cleaner environment and greener transportation. Electric high-speed rail is energy efficient and can carry a lot of people at once. According to the U.S. High Speed Rail Association, "building a high-speed rail system across the U.S. could result in 29 million fewer car trips and 500,000 fewer plane flights each year." The United States passed the High Speed Ground Transportation Act of 1965 to create a national network of high-speed rail. Many state proposals have followed, but one of the most promising projects is in California. A high-speed rail project began there in 2015 to connect Anaheim, San Francisco, and other major cities.

Rail Support Jobs and Duties

While railroad conductors and railroad engineers are two of the most well-known jobs in the industry, there are many other job opportunities for you to consider.

Railroad jobs that involve the safe movement of trains include brake operators, switch operators, signal operators, and dispatchers. Brake operators perform a vital service by coupling and uncoupling train cars, as well as operating some of the train switches. These days, brake operator jobs are being phased out and their duties are handled by the engineer and conductor. Still, this is an important skill to know if you want to advance in the railroad industry.

Signal operators install, repair, and maintain signals along tracks, working mostly outdoors. People in traffic control centers are called dispatchers. They help to direct and control the

A rail yard is a huge parking lot for train cars. This is where trains are stored when they are not being used, undergoing repairs, or preparing for their next trip. Moving trains in and out smoothly takes tremendjous skill and patience.

movement of trains and create systems for managing train traffic in specific, assigned areas.

Other railroad support jobs take place in rail yards, where trains can be loaded, unloaded, stored, or put into position for an upcoming trip without blocking the main rail line. Jobs in rail yards include rail yard engineers, hostlers, and yard masters. Rail yard engineers oversee the movement of train cars from one track to another in preparation for travel to another station. They work to make sure trains stay on schedule by preparing them to move and by fixing any problems with specific cars. Yard masters and hostlers support rail yard engineers in carrying out these duties.

Requirements to Be a Railroad Support Worker

Most railroad support jobs require a high school degree or GED to get started. Railroad companies want their employees to be computer literate, have basic math skills, and have the ability to type at least twenty-five words per minute. If you meet these requirements, you will likely need to attend a training program administered by a railroad company before you can start. The training typically involves hands-on experience.

To work in any of the railroad support jobs like brakeman, yard master, or dispatcher, it is important to understand information that is communicated orally. You will speak with people over a radio, by intercom, or on a telephone. You need to be able to communicate general and technical information clearly and directly, sometimes while you are operating switches at the same time. The ability to multitask is crucial.

People who enjoy fixing things and working outdoors might consider a job as a railway worker. This job involves installing, repairing, and maintaining signals and sections of track.

CHAPTER THREE

On the Road: Ground Transportation

Many people associate roads and highways with freedom and possibility. It has to do with driving down a long stretch of highway, rolling down the windows and feeling the wind whip through your hair, and having the satisfaction of arriving at your destination after many miles. This is one of the many attractions of obtaining a job in the ground transportation sector.

Some transportation workers focus more on moving merchandise, while others are focused on getting people to their destinations. However, all workers in the ground transportation industry share a common goal: to move people, materials, and goods along a road safely and efficiently.

Highways, roads, and streets crisscross much of the world. It took drivers, construction workers, machinists, engineers, bridge architects, city planners, and entrepreneurs to build up what we now call the ground transportation industry.

Truck Drivers, Material Movers, and Parcel Deliverers

Truck drivers pull a lot of weight in the ground transportation industry. Not only do they carry almost 64 percent of all

Eighteen-wheelers often transport goods inside the truck bed so curious people can't see what's inside. Here, there is no guesswork: this truck driver has an important timber delivery to make.

freight imported and exported every year, but without this job, most stores would be completely empty, according to the U.S. Bureau of Transportation Statistics.

There are two main types of truck driver. First, there are truck drivers who drive heavy delivery trucks that have up to eighteen wheels and can carry tons of material, known as big rigs or eighteen-wheelers. These drivers may work for large corporations like Walmart or Costco. Heavy delivery truck drivers move materials from factories to warehouses and stores across the country. They move large loads like cars, produce, cattle, furniture, timber, and gasoline. Heavy truck drivers usually keep long hours and find sleeping accommodations on the road. Staying alert and well rested is one of their biggest challenges. They are sometimes known as long-haul truckers.

The other type of truck driver is called a light or delivery services truck driver. Their vehicles support twenty-six thousand pounds of material or less. Their job is to pick up or deliver merchandise within a specified city area, or do short hauls. Delivery service drivers offer additional services such as collecting payment from customers, giving them their receipts, and maintaining delivery records. Sometimes they use electronic delivery tracking. Route drivers also do similar work but usually along a fixed route within a city. They pick up and deliver things like laundry, flowers, cash for banks, or baked goods.

Both types of truck drivers check fuel levels, brakes, wipers, and signals before leaving on a trip. If there are any problems, they report these to a dispatcher. While they might dedicate some labor to loading and unloading their trucks, most drivers spend the majority of their time behind the wheel.

However goods are otherwise hauled, at some point during their delivery process almost all find their way onto trucks. A whole other category of ground transportation worker handles moving material on and off trucks: material movers. They work closely with truck drivers, and also operate loading and unloading equipment, such as cranes, forklifts, and bulldozers. They often work inside warehouses or factories.

Parcel Delivery

Parcel delivery is another big business within the ground transportation industry. Parcels are packages that people mail to another person or company located in different, usually distant, locations. Parcel deliverers ensure that packages arrive at their destinations on time. Time management, good driving ability, and physical fitness are all prerequisites for a successful parcel delivery person.

UPS and FedEx are two well-known parcel delivery services in the United States, with the average worker on a route making over 150–200 delivery stops per day.

Well-known parcel delivery companies include FedEx, UPS, and USPS. Large Internet companies like Amazon and eBay also rely on parcel delivery to carry out their business. All of these companies need people to sort, package, weigh, sell postage, organize, and deliver packages. Even though trucks and vans are most often used for parcel delivery, these companies sometimes also use planes, trains, or boats to make sure their deliveries arrive on time.

Veteran female commercial driver's license trainer Kay Burton (*second from left*) instructs trainees in hitching techniques during a 2014 CDL class in Mt. Sterling, Kentucky.

Ground Transportation: What It Takes

It takes independence, self-control, and consistency to be a truck driver. Truckers spend a lot of time on the road by themselves. If you tend to be an introvert—that is, if your energy is recharged when you spend time alone—you might like this job. You have lots of time to listen to music, audiobooks, and the radio when you are driving on an open highway. Truckers also need to be flexible and adaptable. They often encounter changes in weather, traffic patterns, or delivery schedules.

Becoming a truck driver, parcel deliverer, or material mover requires at least a high school diploma or GED. To operate a large eighteen-wheel truck, it takes training, certification, and a special license called a commercial driver's license (CDL). To drive all other types of trucks, you only need a regular driver's license. Many vocational-technical schools offer CDL training and licensing assistance.

You need to be at least twenty-one years old to make deliveries to other states. Some states allow drivers as young as eighteen to make deliveries within state borders. Look up the Federal Motor Carrier Safety Regulations to find out what's required where you live. Whichever type of truck you

THE RISE OF THE AUTOMOBILE AND THE INTERSTATE HIGHWAY SYSTEM

The first automobiles began rattling along dirt roads in North America back in the early 1900s. Since then, people have continued to use and improve vehicles and roads. As cars became more popular, they began to grow in size to fit more people and materials inside. Instead of just a four-passenger automobile, engineers developed vans, pick-up trucks, buses, and eventually vehicles as large as eighteen-wheel trucks. From 1956 to the 1990s, the United States saw a huge growth in the number of paved streets, roads, and bridges under the 1956 Federal-Aid Highway Act (NSSGA, 2016). This made it possible for vehicles to get around cities, to move from city to city, and even to drive all the way from coast to coast on one very long road called an interstate highway. The interstate highway is over forty-six thousand miles (long. Today on the interstate, you will see antique cars from the 1900s all the way to cutting-edge green electric cars.

A school bus driver inspects and prepares her bus in the early morning hours. She is responsible for the safety of the bus and of the children she is about to transport.

are interested in driving, it is very helpful to study subjects like mathematics, computers, electronics, and automotive mechanics to prepare for a truck-driving career.

Bus, Taxi, and Limo Drivers

Bus drivers move people from one place to another along a fixed route. Bus drivers work for public and private schools, city bus systems, colleges, universities, and tourism companies. They drive a variety of routes in small areas, and also long journeys.

Bus drivers should have a good sense of direction and know how to find new routes if there are delays in traffic due to construction or accidents. Some bus drivers work for tourism companies and transport passengers long distances for sightseeing or vacation.

Becoming a bus driver is a good choice for someone who enjoys people and routine. In fact, bus drivers who work with children and older adults tend to be very compassionate and friendly people. Schoolchildren benefit from a reassuring bus driver. Aging citizens sometimes stop driving themselves and take advantage of transportation alternatives, especially those with disabilities. If you are good with older people and think you'd find satisfaction helping them continue to have a high quality of life by getting them out to doctor appointments, shopping, or to fun excursions, then being a bus driver for the elderly would be a very satisfying choice for you.

Taxi and Livery Drivers

Taxi drivers take people to the places they need to go. Unlike bus drivers, they take clients or customers to their requested destinations. Taxi drivers usually work in big cities, where fewer people own cars, or where public transportation is infrequent or inconvenient, or shut down (such as at night).

Internet-based ride request service companies such as Uber and Lyft have become hugely popular. Using a smartphone app, a person can request a ride with a nearby driver. These drivers use their private vehicles and choose where and how often they work. It is a great way to make some extra cash on the side, or it can be a full-time gig.

While taxi drivers usually take people to specific destinations, chauffeurs usually drive for set periods of time in luxury vehicles, either as rentals, or for specific clients. For example, wedding parties often hire chauffeurs for the whole day to take the bride, groom, and all of their friends and family from the wedding ceremony to the reception in a nice limousine.

Good driving records are a top priority for taxi drivers. Frederick Amoafo, shown here, has driven over fifty thousand miles without an accident and was declared New York's Safest Cabbie in 2014.

What You Need to Drive

Many companies require a high school diploma or GED for drivers they hire. Drivers should be people and service oriented and know how to operate systems and equipment. It is good to have basic math or accounting skills to maintain your own income records. A proven record of safe and successful driving is essential. This means studying driver's education, obtaining a license, and driving responsibly. Doing these things will convince future employers that you are safe and reliable.

Float On: Water Transportation

People who work in water transportation love being on or near the water. They get to experience the wonders of oceans, rivers, lakes, gulfs, canals, waterways, and bays. Many exciting job opportunities exist in water transportation. From large ocean cruise liners, to small commuter ferries, to cargo ships, water transportation workers perform vital services every day.

Water transportation industry workers experience both challenges and benefits. One of the main challenges of working in this industry is dealing with extreme and abrupt changes in weather conditions. However, with the right skills and experience, you can learn how to deal with these challenges and focus your attention on the benefits. Big benefits like working in a sustainable field, earning a reliable income, and having adventures on the high seas can be yours if you pursue a career in water transportation industry.

Making a Big Splash: Jobs in Water Transportation

Workers in water transportation operate a variety of vessels to move people and cargo. They travel to foreign ports or along local inland waterways, loading and unloading their boats along the way. As with the other transportation industries, jobs in water transportation can be divided into two categories: transporting materials and transporting people.

Onboard: Jobs and Duties

Water cargo and passengers are transported on a variety of ships and boats. Larger vessels include cruise liners, tankers, deep-sea container carriers, and bulk carriers. Midsize to smaller vessels include barges, tugboats, ferries, luxury yachts,

A boat captain pulls a tugboat out to sea. Tugboats push or tow vessels that need some help and guidance, such as getting through a crowded harbor.

sailboats, and motorboats. Larger vessels carry imports and exports. Some of the most frequently imported items shipped to North America include iron ore, coal, clay, lumber, and petroleum. Frequent exports out of North America to other countries include all kinds of agricultural products—wheat, corn, barley, soy, and forest products, to name a few. Smaller vessels tend to carry only people. For example, ferries carry people across rivers. Larger ferries are sturdy enough to allow many people to drive onboard inside their cars.

The Staten Island Ferry transports people from Staten Island to Lower Manhattan. Ferries are a tremendous help to commuters in areas with lots of waterways. They are also good for those who work on the water but want to reside in a city.

Chain of Command

Jobs in water transportation require workers to operate and maintain a water vessel, make sure it is safe, load and unload it, and follow strict chains of command. The job duties and chain of command on board a ship change depending on the type of water vessel. For example, a large deep-sea container vessel is operated by a big crew of merchant marines. Above deck there is a captain who is supported by three mates. At least three sailors, also called deckhands, support the captain and mates. Below deck there is a chief engineer and three assistant engineers. The assistant engineers are equivalent in rank to the three mates above deck. They are usually supported by two or three marine oilers who are equivalent in rank to the sailors above deck.

If you have been counting, this is at least thirteen positions on a large ship, and that is not including other workers like the cooks, carpenters, electricians, and mechanics who also work on large ships. In contrast, on a smaller boat like a piloted motorboat there may only be one or two people who perform all of the duties assigned to these thirteen workers. What exactly is involved in these various positions?

Above Deck

The captain is the person in charge of the water vessel. The boat captain is responsible for the safety and well-being of the various crew members on the ship. Boat captains supervise the crew and their procedures, maintain a budget, oversee the boarding and unboarding of passengers, and interact with the passengers. If the boat is transporting cargo, the captain oversees the loading and unloading of it. The boat captain also communicates with the chief engineer below deck about the boat's speed.

Up to three mates support a boat captain. The first mate usually oversees the boat's cargo and has the most authority. The second mate is in charge of navigation and speed, while the third mate ensures safety. Sailors support the captain and mates. The head sailor is called a boatswain. New sailors are sometimes called ordinary seamen, and experienced sailors are called able seamen. Don't let the word "men" in these traditional job titles fool you. Many women work in the water transportation industry these days, too.

Under the boatswain's direction, the sailors perform routine maintenance on deck, keep watch for obstacles and weather conditions, help with boat's docking and departing, inspect cargo, monitor the boat's position, check its speed and direction, and make announcements based on information gathered from these activities. For example, one of the most famous announcements that sailors make is "Land, ahoy!" This means the

A crew of commercial sailors work with ropes on board. The combined efforts of sailors and ship officers are needed to move boats and ships around safely and efficiently.

sailor has just spotted land and is announcing this to crew so that they can take action.

Boat pilots help large ships that are passing through local waterways or that are docking temporarily in local harbors. They operate smaller motorboats and board large ships using ladders. They then communicate with the boat's captain, mates, and sailors to get the ship into the harbor or safely through the waterway and back on the open sea. Boat pilots have a high level of local knowledge about their area's tides, currents, and other special considerations that a ship's crew, who is just passing through, would not likely know.

Below Deck

The ship's engine is located below deck. It takes many people to operate and maintain ship engines. A chief engineer usually heads all operations below deck, running the engine room and being responsible for the ship's propulsion, or forward movement. Propulsion is made possible when engine, boilers, generators, pumps, and other machinery work together. To assist, the chief engineer works with up to three assistant engineers. The assistant engineers do anything from electrical wiring, refrigeration, and ventilation to starting the engine and adjusting the speed based on the captain's orders. They also help with calculating fuel needs and keeping inventory of all the machine parts in the engine room.

Marine oilers also work in the engine room and report to the assistant engineers. Their main duty is to keep the propulsion system up and running. A new marine oiler is sometimes called a wiper, while an experienced marine oiler can earn a credential called a QMED, or Qualified Member of the Engine Department. They help with repairs and lubrication of engine room machinery, maintain hoses and pumps, read and inter-pret temperature and pressure gauges, maintain gears and shafts, and sometimes help sailors above deck with loading and unloading cargo.

What It's Really Like: Above and Below Deck

The type of boat you work on determines a lot about your work experience in the water transportation industry. Larger vessels head to deep ocean waters and require you to be

A ship's engine is located below deck and powers, or propels, the ship forward. Propulsion is achieved when the engine, boilers, generators, pumps, and other machinery work together.

DOCKWORKERS

Dockworkers, sometimes called longshoremen or stevedores, help to load and unload cargo from a ship onto the dock. Dockworkers need to have a high school diploma or GED and be at least eighteen years old. Their job duties vary depending on the type of cargo they are handling.

Containerization. Large container ships use a process called containerization in which standard-sized containers are filled with a product and then sealed. Dockworkers specialize in sealing, unsealing, loading, and unloading these containers.

Nonstandard cargo. Other dockworkers specialize in moving nonstandard-sized cargo like cars and scrap metal. They may need to use power winches, forklifts, powerful magnets, or hooks to move these items.

Liquids. If the cargo is liquid, dockworkers often use large hoses to unload it. Liquids like oil, molasses, vegetable oils, or chemicals are loaded onto ships through hoses.

away from home for two to three months at a time. These longer voyages can take their toll on a crew. They endure cramped quarters, long hours away from their families, and sometimes injury or danger as they perform their duties out in the rough elements.

On the other hand, companies that want to attract good talent have begun to offer more perks, like spacious living quarters, on-ship cooks, air-conditioning, TV, and Internet to make the long months fly by. The peace and quiet and proximity to nature are also selling points. Smaller vessels tend to work inland along waterways, rivers, or harbors. Workers on these vessels might run the boat for seven or eight hours a day, but then they can go home at night.

Ship Workers

To work in the water transportation industry, customer service, physical skills, and mechanical skills are vital. Customer service involves being able to communicate with people effectively to determine their needs and then know how to meet those needs. Physical requirements include having good sight and hearing, including good hand-eye coordination, and being able to lift heavy loads. It also helps to have a strong stomach; you should not be not prone to seasickness. Workers on ships need to have a good understanding of machinery, engines, and electrical systems.

Dockworkers get a container ready to be elevated onto a container ship. Their job is to load and unload cargo from ships onto the dock, and vice versa.

Most deck mates, engineers, and boat pilots earn a bachelor's degree from a merchant marine academy. These academies typically offer the degree in combination with a MMC, a Merchant Marine Credential. Almost every water transportation worker also earns a TWIC, or Transportation Worker Identification Card. You might have to take a written exam to earn this credential if you have a higher position aboard a ship.

Degrees and certifications aside, there is nothing like on-the-job experience. In fact, specific years of experience allow workers to advance a level. For example, for every 365 days of service as a crew member above deck on a ship, a worker can earn an endorsement to advance one level. Similarly, workers who start out as deck crew and who remain on the job for three to four years can advance to deck mates and eventually even to captain, without having ever attending a merchant marine academy.

Let's Roll: Pursuing Your Ideal Job in the Transportation Industry

A world of possibility awaits someone hoping to work in the transportation industry. Deciding what you want to do is the first and sometimes the most difficult part. With so many options, however, it can be hard to choose. Figuring out your strengths and what you want out of a job (besides a monetary livelihood) will help you decide. Armed with some tips on job search skills, and how to apply and interview for work, you will be well on your way to landing your ideal job in this dynamic and important employment sector.

Making a Decision

Most schools employ guidance counselors to assist students with academic and personal concerns, and to provide help with career decisions and planning. If you are struggling to decide on a career path, your school guidance counselor can help you isolate your strengths and interests.

People generally find satisfaction doing work that fits their interests. After you have determined your best skills and

Many jobs in transportation require specialized and extensive training. Here, two students at a helicopter pilot program get some pointers from the instructor.

abilities, you can create a list of job types that suit you. For example, if you like driving, then becoming a professional bus or truck driver could be good options. If you are mechanically minded, a locomotive engineer position might be in your future. The proper educational credentials differ for each job, though most entry-level jobs require only a high school diploma or GED.

What jobs are available? Find out by conducting job searches. in a variety of places. Check online at employment websites, read school and public library resources, call and e-mail employers, and network with people who know workers in the transportation industry.

Online Searches

Getting online, for many people, is as easy as walking over to a computer or whipping out a phone. But even those without home Internet access are not out of luck. Most public libraries have a computer lab where you can search the Internet and use word-processing programs to work on résumés and cover letters. The reference librarian can also help you find resources with job listings. Many cities and towns also have state labor offices with computer labs for job seekers. They also offer help finding information on training and certifications that are needed for the jobs that most interest you. Counselors are usually available to help, too.

To get a job in the transportation industry, you need experience. If you don't yet have on-the-job experience, then the next best thing is to get unpaid experience, like these volunteer movers.

Employment websites like Indeed, Monster, CareerBuilder, Simply Hired, Snagajob, AOL Jobs, Dice, JobBankUSA, and EmploymentGuide are a safe bet, listing opportunities in many different industries. For a more specific search focusing on the transportation industry, consider identifying specific companies and visiting their websites to check their openings. Top airline companies include American Airlines, Air Canada, and Delta. Major rail companies include CSX and Union Pacific, while corporations like Walmart, Target, Home Depot, and K-Mart, hire ground and water transportation workers. Don't forget about parcel delivery companies such as FedEx, UPS, DHL, and others.

Networking

Talking to people employed in this sector is another good strategy. In other words: networking. You may be surprised by the opportunities that arise when you go beyond waiting for people and jobs to come to you, and become proactive.

Websites like LinkedIn focus on professional networking, but you can also connect with your own social network: friends, relatives, teachers, guidance counselors, or even your current employer if you have a job now. You might also consider talking to classmates or people you meet when you are doing hobbies. People in your after-school activities, like sports or music lessons, are also potential resources for your job search. Even if they do not know someone offhand currently, they may very well remember you later if they hear of something down the road.

Applying Yourself

Applying for a job may involve filling out an application, providing a résumé that lists your qualifications, and writing a cover letter that promotes yourself as the perfect candidate for the job. Some jobs require testing and some combination of these other requirements. An interview is the last step in the job search process.

It is hard work to follow these steps to complete two or three, let alone five to ten, job applications. In fact, finding work is its own full-time job. However, the hard work and dedication are well worth the effort. .

When you find a job that you want to apply for, the first thing you will need to do is to read the job description carefully. Envision yourself performing the duties that are listed. How do you feel when you imagine yourself doing these things? Do the duties match your skills, interests, and abilities? If you get a positive feeling and can clearly seeing yourself doing these job duties, then you are on the right track.

A typical job application asks you to provide basic contact information and details about your education and past work experience. If you don't have past work experience, then you can list volunteer activities and life experiences that directly relate to the skills needed for the job. For example, if you have ever worked at a restaurant, then you have picked up

Job fairs are an excellent place to learn about employment opportunities and to share your résumé with professionals. This job fair brought together Chinese airlines with prospective pilots and others.

excellent people skills. The same is true if you volunteered serving food to homeless people at a local soup kitchen. Many employers want to know that you can relate to people and communicate effectively. Both the restaurant and soup kitchen experiences would prove that you have people skills, a skill that you could include on your résumé.

The Right Résumé

A résumé is a list of your most pertinent education, past work experience, key skills, activities, and awards that relate to the job you are applying for. The résumé should list certifications you have earned. You might have to change your résumé depending on the job you are applying for. For example, if you want to work as a flight attendant, it would be more important communication and people skills. If you want to work as a car mechanic, then it would be more important to highlight your technical skills. Writing a cover letter will allow you to explain your most important skills in more detail. A cover letter is addressed directly to the employer and explains more fully why you are a good candidate for the job. Highlight your most recent professional experience and any academic awards in a cover letter, while avoiding simply repeating the information listed in your résumé.

When completing the application, résumé, and cover letter, it is important to keep key words and phrases in mind from the job description. You want to use these words if they can honestly describe your skills and experience. For example, many job descriptions in the transportation industry list physical abilities such as "able to lift heavy weights of at least fifty pounds." If you were a high school athlete, then you might list this under the activities section of your résumé, for example.

Don't get frustrated if you have completed several job applications and are still waiting for an interview. This is a normal part of the job search process. It usually takes several applications before you are contacted. The applications you filled out are not wasted effort. Completing multiple applications helps you to zero in on your strengths, weaknesses, and interests. The clearer these qualities are in your mind, the more confident you will feel during an interview.

Interviewing

An interview is your opportunity to meet an employer face-to-face and to convince him or her to hire you. It is important to dress as professionally as possible for an interview, even if your job will not be in an office. It is recommended that men

AIR TRANSPORTATION RÉSUMÉS

Your résumé will look different depending on the type of job you are applying for in the air transportation industry. If you want to get a job as a pilot, it's important to include the total number of flight hours, or hours you have flown in the air, that you have achieved to date. Make sure to mention how many of those hours you were the pilot in command. The cover letter will stress your key qualities, like being detail oriented and being able to handle an airplane even in hazardous circumstances. You might include an example of how you successfully managed one of these stressful situations such as an emergency landing, or a seemingly never-ending delay. However, if you are most interested in getting a job as an airport worker, it is more important to focus on your customer service skills and ability to work with people in the résumé and cover letter.

Shaking hands and making eye contact are basic steps and rituals necessary to the process of interviewing for any job. Many jobs in transportation require good communication and interpersonal skills.

wear a jacket and tie, slacks, a button-up collared shirt, and nice dress shoes. Women can wear similar clothing as well as a skirt suit or nice dress with a blazer on top. Both men and women should cover up tattoos and remove jewelry in piercings for an interview.

Find out as much as you can about the workplace a few days before the interview. This includes figuring out the location of the interview and the best route to get to it. Test out the route a few days ahead of time so that you are calm when you arrive for your interview. Prepare a list of questions your employer is likely to ask you and how you might answer. Even though you are the person being interviewed, it is also a good idea to prepare a list of questions you have about the job to ask your interviewer. This shows confidence and commitment.

During the interview process, it is important to make eye contact, offer a firm handshake when greeting and leaving, speak clearly, and accentuate the positive. It is best to avoid inappropriate jokes, to speak negatively about past jobs or employers, or to talk about salary too early in the interview process.

Once you are offered the job, then that is the appropriate time to negotiate a salary that would satisfy you. After the interview, it is highly recommended that you send a thank-you letter to the person who interviewed you. This shows your interest in the job and appreciation for the interviewer's valuable time.

The Job Offer

An employer may offer you the job at the end of the interview. More often, an offer will come via a phone call or an e-mail a few days (and even weeks) afteward. Whichever way you receive the job offer—Contratulations! Your hard work paid off.

If you really want the job, the only thing left is to answer with an affirmative yes. If you need time to think it over, write or call back with your thanks, and a request for a few hours or a couple of days to decide. Make sure, of course, that they do not need an answer right away. You don't want to lose your opportunity through indecision.

If you need time, weigh the pros and cons of the job and discuss the opportunity with close family and friends, especially if the job requires that you relocate or make certain time commitments. You may even be waiting for another response from another employer before you commit.

First Days of Work and Beyond

Whether your new job is in air, rail, ground, or water transportation, it is important to make a good impression on the first day of work. Show up on time, wearing the appropriate clothes for the job. Bring a positive attitude and willingness to dive right in, working and learning the ropes.

Not only will you learn new procedures, but you will also meet your new coworkers. Take time to learn their names and their positions so that you know who to go to in the days to come when you have questions or need help. It is great to make friends and have a sense of camaraderie at work, but you also want to keep things professional, especially with your supervisor and company directors. Avoid bad language, off-color jokes, or any negative remarks about race, gender, religion, or sexual orientation.

During your first days of work, you may attend training sessions, workplace orientation meetings with other new hires, and meetings with your boss(es). You will fill out human resources (HR) paperwork, and may receive an employee handbook that covers workplace procedures.

As a new hire, you will likely be given your own space—an office, cubicle, locker, or even a truck depending on the job. It is important to keep your assigned space and equipment neat and working properly, and your uniforms in good condition. You might also be assigned to a more senior or experienced worker as your mentor.

Take advantage of your status as a new hire and ask lots of questions. As a new hire, it is more acceptable to have lots of questions and maybe even make a few mistakes as opposed to someone who has been on the job for six months or more. Your employer won't expect you to know how to do everything your first day, so relax and enjoy the learning process.

If you follow these guidelines, you will be well on your way to a fulfilling career in the transportation industry. Job searches, applications, interviews, and first days on the job are just the beginning. Soon enough you will be flying through the air, chugging along a railroad track, bussing through a busy city route, or sailing on the ocean. The transportation industry will continue to change as engineers and technicians find new and improved ways to move goods and people around. At the same time, it is a stable yet dynamic and exciting industry with promising job growth and salary potential for the future. It's a big world out there, and you can start seeing it if you pursue a job in the transportation industry.

altitude The vertical distance from the ground at which an aircraft flies.

cargo Goods or merchandise carried on a ship, airplane, or vehicle.

coupling In rail transportation, this is the connecting and unconnecting of railroad cars.

cover letter A letter written to a potential employer highlighting your qualifications for the job.

deck The top platform of a ship.

extrovert Someone who enjoys spending many hours with other people socializing.

flight record An official document maintained by a pilot that includes detailed information about each takeoff, flight, and landing of an aircraft.

freight Goods to be transported from one place to another; similar to "cargo" and used in all types of transportation work, but most commonly used in railroad transportation.

hangar The space where airplanes are stored when they are not in use or when they are being repaired.

interstate A system of expressways connecting most major U.S. cities.

introvert Someone who enjoys many hours spent independently listening to music, reading, or thinking.

limousine A large, luxurious automobile, especially one driven by a chauffeur who is separated from the passengers by a partition.

locomotive A self-propelled vehicle that runs on rails and is used for moving railroad cars.

mentor An experienced person who teaches and guides a less experienced person through a particular trade, job, or career choice.

multitasking The ability to do several activities at the same time such as making an announcement while operating a digital control.

parcel A wrapped package or bundle that is delivered from one person or company to another; it is usually transported a good distance before it arrives at its destination.

perseverance The ability to continue a project or enterprise despite challenges and setbacks.

proactive Creating or controlling a situation by causing something to happen rather than passively responding to it after it has happened.

propulsion The action of driving or pushing something forward, such as a vehicle.

résumé A list of a job candidate's education, work experience, awards, affiliations, and certifications.

runway The long strip of paved road designed specifically for departing and landing aircraft

transportation The public movement of passengers or goods in air, ground, rail, or water.

vessel A ship, boat, or other object designed to float on water while carrying goods and passengers.

FOR MORE INFORMATION

American Public Transportation Association
1300 I Street NW
Suite 1200 East
Washington, DC 20005
(202) 496-4800
Website: http://www.apta.com
This professional organization is concerned with strength-
ening and improving public transportation through
advocacy, innovation, and information sharing; it works to
ensure that public transportation is available and accessible for all communities across the country.

American Trucking Associations
950 North Glebe Road, Suite 210
Arlington, VA 22203-4181
(703) 838-1700
Website: http://www.trucking.org
This professional organization is committed to developing
and advocating innovative, research-based policies that
promote highway safety, security, environmental sustain-
ability, and profitability.

Association of American Railroads
425 3rd Street SW
Washington, DC 20024
(202) 639-2100
Website: https://www.aar.org/Pages/Careers.aspx
This association is focused on ensuring that railroads remain
safe, efficient, cost-effective, and environmentally sound.
It offers standard setting, industry data, and professional
networking.

Canadian Transportation Agency
15 Eddy Street
Gatineau, Quebec J8X 4B3
Canada
(888) 222-2592
Website: https://www.otc-cta.gc.ca/eng
This agency makes decisions and determinations on a wide
range of matters involving air, rail, and marine modes of
transportation under the authority of parliament.

Federal Aviation Administration
800 Independence Avenue, SW, Room 908
Washington, DC 20591
(202) 267-3883
Website: http://www.faa.gov
This governmental division's mission is to provide the safest,
most efficient aerospace system in the world.

Federal Maritime Commission
800 North Capitol Street, NW
Washington, DC 20573
(202) 523-5807
Website: http://www.fmc.gov
This commission is the federal agency responsible for regu-
lating the U.S. international ocean transportation system
for the benefit of U.S. exporters, importers, and the U.S.
consumer.

Federal Railroad Administration
1200 New Jersey Avenue, SE
Washington, DC 20590

(202) 493-6014

Website: https://www.fra.dot.gov

The Federal Railroad Administration (FRA) was created by the Department of Transportation Act of 1966. It is one of ten agencies within the U.S. Department of Transportation concerned with intermodal transportation.

Human Resources and Skills Development Canada (HRSDC)

Service Canada Canada Enquiry Centre

Ottawa, ON K1A 0J9

Canada

(800) 563-5677

Website: http://www.hrsdc.gc.ca/eng/home.shtml

A division of the Canadian government, HRSDC is committed to career help for Canadian citizens. It provides job assistance, career advice, and a number of other services.

U.S. Department of Labor

Frances Perkins Building

200 Constitution Avenue NW

Washington, DC 20210

(866) 4-USA-DOL

Website: http://www.dol.gov

The Department of Labor's mission is to foster, promote, and develop the welfare of the wage earners, job seekers, and retirees of the United States; improve working conditions; advance opportunities for profitable employment; and assure work-related benefits and rights.

U.S. Department of Transportation
1200 New Jersey Avenue, SE
Washington, DC 20590
(855) 368-4200
Website: https://www.transportation.gov
The mission of the department is to ensure a fast, safe, efficient, accessible, and convenient transportation system that meets national interests and enhances quality of life.

Websites

Because of the changing number of Internet links, Rosen Publishing has developed an online list of websites related to the subject of this book. This site is updated regularly. Please use this link to access this list:

http://www.rosenlinks.com/JOBS/trans

Craig, Joe. *The Vo-Tech Track to Success in Manufacturing, Mechanics, and Automotive Care.* New York, NY: Rosen Publishing, 2014.

Crawford, Matthew B. *Shop Class as Soulcraft: An Inquiry into the Value of Work.* New York: Penguin Books, 2010.

Dolan, Edward. *Careers in the U.S. Air Force.* New York, NY: Cavendish Square Publishing, 2009.

Dolan, Edward. *Careers in the U.S. Coast Guard.* New York, NY: Cavendish Square Publishing, 2009.

Doyle, Allison. *Internet Your Way to a New Job.* Cupertino, CA: Happy About, 2011.

Grensing-Prophal, Lin. *The Everything Résumé Book.* Avon, MA: Adams Media, 2012.

Hemingway, Meghan and Mulder, Kara. *The Flight Attendant Life Careers Workbook: The Face-To-Face Interview.* Amazon Digital Services, 2015.

Hill, Paul. *The Panic Free Job Search: Unleash the Power of the Web and Social Networking to Get Hired.* Pompton Plains, NJ: Career Press, 2012.

JIST Works, Eds. *Young Person's Occupational Outlook Handbook, 6th Ed.* Indianapolis, IN: 2007

Jones, Molly. *21st Century Education and Careers: Options and Strategies.* New York, NY: Rosen Publishing, 2012

Krannich, Caryl and Ron. *Job Interview Tips for People with Not-So-Hot Backgrounds: How to Put Red Flags Behind you to Win the Job.* Manassas Park, VA: Impact Publications, 2004.

Loomis, Jim. All Aboard: *The Complete North American Train Travel Guide.* Chicago, IL: Chicago Review Press, 2015.

Mason, Helen. *Urban Planner.* New York, NY: Gareth Stevens Publishing, 2014.

Otfinoski, Steven. *High-Speed Trains: From Concept to Consumer.* (Calling All Innovators: A Career for You). New York, NY: C. Press/F. Watts Trade Education Books, 2015.

Souter, Janet. *Air Marshal and Careers in Transportation Security.* New York, NY: Enslow Publishing, 2006.

Whiteman, Lily. *How to Land a Top-Paying Federal Job: Your Complete Guide to Opportunities, Internships, Résumés and Cover Letters, Networking, Interviews, Salaries, Promotions, and More!* New York, NY: American Management Association, 2012.

American School Counselor Association. "What Does a School Guidance Counselor Do?" Retrieved January 11, 2016 (www.schoolcounselor.org/press/what-does-a-school-counselor-do).

Blanchard, Dave. "U.S. Logistics: Slow Growth Is Good Growth in the Era of the New Normal." *Material Handling & Logistics*. August 2013.

Bureau of Transportation Statistics. "April 2015 North American Freight Numbers." U.S. Department of Transportation. April 2015. Retrieved January 7, 2016 (http://www.rita.dot.gov/bts/press_releases/bts031_15).

Bureau of Transportation Statistics. "Transportation Services Index." November 2015. Retrieved January 7, 2016 (http://www.rita.dot.gov/bts/transportation_services_index).

CareerOneStop. "Occupation Profile: Transportation, Storage, and Distribution Managers." Retrieved January 18, 2016 (http://www.careerinfonet.org/occ_rep.asp?next=occ_rep&Level=&optstatus=111111111&jobfam=29&id=1&nodeid=2&soccode=113071&menuMode=&stfips=35&x=32&y=10).

Dakers, Diane. *Green Ways of Getting Around: Careers in Transportation (Green-Collar Careers)*. New York, NY: Crabtree Publishing Company, 2011.

Encyclopedia of Careers and Vocational Guidance, Fourteenth Edition. New York, NY: Infobase Publishing, 2008.

Hu, Patricia. "TSI Measures More Than the Number of Trucks on the Road." Retrieved January 17, 2016 (https://www.transportation.gov/fastlane/tsi-measures-more-number-trucks-road).

Institute for Career Research. *A Career as an Aircraft Mechanic.* Amazon Digital Services: 2014.

JIST Works. *200 Best Jobs for Renewing America.* Indianapolis, IN: JIST Publishing, 2010.

JIST Works. *Nontraditional Careers: Guide to Nontraditional Occupations for Women and for Men.* Indianapolis, IN: JIST Publishing, 2011.

Lichtenstein, Nelson, Ed. *WAL-MART: The Face of Twenty-First Century Capitalism.* New York, NY: The New Press, 2006.

McKinney, Anne. *Real Résumés for Aviation and Travel Jobs.* Fayetteville, NC: Prep Publishing, 2002.

NSSGA. "History of the Federal Aid Highway Program." Retrieved January 14, 2016 (http://www.nssga.org/advocacy/grass-roots/reauthorization-roadmap/history-federal-aid-highway-program).

Powers, Paul. *Winning Job Interviews.* Franklin Lakes, NJ: Career Press, 2010.

U.S. Bureau of Transportation Statistics. *U.S. Department of Transportation.* "Growth in the Nation's Freight Statistics." Retrieved January 10, 2016 (http://www.rita.dot.gov/bts/sites/rita.dot.gov.bts/files/publications/freight_shipments_in_america/html/entire.html).

U.S. Department of Labor. *Occupational Outlook Handbook: 2014–2015.* New York, NY: Skyhorse Publishing, 2014.

U.S. Department of Transportation. *Freight in America: A New National Picture.* Washington, DC: Research and Innovative Technology Administration, 2006.

U.S. Department of Transportation. *Maritime Trade and Transportation.* Washington, DC: Research and Innovative Technology Administration, 2007.

Warren, Roxanne. *Rail and the City.* Cambridge, MA: The MIT Press, 2014.

Weingroff, Richard R. "The Year of the Interstate." fhwa.dot. gov. Retrieved January 2, 2016 (https://www.fhwa.dot. gov/publications/publicroads/06jan/01.cfm).

World Economic Forum. "Outlook on the Logistics and Supply Chain Industry." Retrieved December 18, 2015 (http://www3.weforum.org/docs/WEF_GAC_ LogisticsSupplyChainSystems_Outlook_2013.pdf).

About the Author

Katherine Yaun has a Master's degree in English and teaches international students at a university in Florida. She is also a writer and editor and has covered many topics in her career including urban development, employment, language acquisition, and postsecondary education.

Katherine comes from a long line of transportation workers. The daughter of an air traffic controller and flight attendant, granddaughter of a pilot and airplane/automobile mechanic, she has fond memories of their tales from out in the field. She is happy to share what she has learned in her first Rosen publication.

Photo Credits